Why Why Why are lions lazy?

Miles Kelly PUBLISHING

First published in 2008 by
Miles Kelly Publishing Ltd
Bardfield Centre, Great Bardfield, Essex, CM7 4SL

Copyright © Miles Kelly Publishing Ltd 2008

2 4 6 8 10 9 7 5 3 1

Editorial Director
Belinda Gallagher

Art Director
Jo Brewer

Editorial Assistant
Carly Blake

Volume Designer
Sally Lace

Indexer
Hilary Bird

Production Manager
Elizabeth Brunwin

Reprographics
Anthony Cambray, Ian Paulyn

ISBN 978-1-84810-035-0

Printed in China

British Library Cataloguing-in-Publication Data
A catalogue record for this book is available
from the British Library

www.mileskelly.net
info@mileskelly.net

www.factsforprojects.com

Contents

What is the biggest cat?

The Siberian tiger is the biggest cat, and one of the largest meat-eating animals in the world. The heaviest Siberian tiger was recorded at weighing 465 kilograms – that's the same weight as 23 of you! It also has thick fur to help it survive in freezing conditions.

Where do tigers live?

Tigers only live in southern and eastern Asia, in forests, woodlands and swamps. They used to live in much larger areas, but humans have now built houses and farms on much of the land. Siberian tigers live in snow-covered forests where temperatures can be -50°C.

Siberian tiger

Hair-head!

Male lion cubs begin to grow thick fur around their head and neck at about three years old. This fur is called a mane.

Why do lion cubs have to leave home?

Male lion cubs don't get to stay with their family group or pride, they get pushed out at about three years old. By then they are old enough to look after themselves. Soon they will take over new prides and have their own cubs.

Discover

Tigers are only found in certain parts of the world. Look on a map and see if you can find them.

What is a caracal?

A caracal is a smaller type of wild cat that lives in hot, dry desert-like places. It hunts small animals, such as rats and hares, and can leap up to 3 metres high to catch a passing bird.

Caracal

Think
Jaguars are good swimmers. Can you think of some other animals that can swim?

Why do tiger cubs have to hide?

Tiger cubs hide behind their mothers for safety. Adult male tigers will kill any cubs that aren't their own. Less than half of the tiger cubs born in the wild live to the age of two years old.

Jaguar

Are jaguars good swimmers?

Jaguars are very good swimmers. Of all cats, they are the most water-loving. They like to live in swampy areas or places that flood during the rainy season, and they enjoy cooling off in rivers. Jaguars are mainly found in Central and South America.

Tiny kitty!

The black-footed cat of southern Africa is one of the smallest cats in the world. It's half the size of many pet cats.

Do big cats live in groups?

Lions are the only big cats that live in large family groups, called 'prides'. A pride is normally made up of four to six female lions, one or two males and their cubs. Some prides may have up to 30 animals if there is plenty of food nearby.

Pride of lions →

Pretend

Imagine you are a prowling lion creeping up on your prey. See how slowly and quietly you can move.

Which cats can scream?

Small cats such as pumas make an ear-piercing scream instead of a roar. The cat family can be divided into two groups — big cats that can roar, and small cats that can't. A screaming cat can still be just as frightening!

Lady-lion hunt!

Female lions, called lionesses, do nearly all of the hunting for the pride. Male lions will only help with the hunt if it's a big animal such as a buffalo or a giraffe.

Why are lions lazy?

Lions seem very lazy, but they have to rest to keep cool in the hot African sun. Usually, lions rest for around 20 hours a day. Hunting normally happens in the morning or at night when it's coolest, and once a lion has had a meal it doesn't need to eat again for several days.

Why are tigers stripy?

Tigers are stripy to help them blend into their shadowy, leafy surroundings. Stripes also help to hide the shape of the tiger's body, making hunting easier. White tigers born in the wild are less likely live as long as orange tigers because they do not blend in as well.

Tiger cubs

Going, gone!

It's too late for some big cats. The Taiwan clouded leopard, and the Caspian, Bali and Javan tigers are extinct (have died out).

Which cat is in danger?

The Iberian lynx, found in Spain and Portugal, is the most endangered cat. This is because humans have cut down many forests where they live. Lynx numbers are also falling because of the drop in the number of rabbits, which are their main food.

Iberian lynx

What do ocelots eat?

Ocelots, also called 'painted leopards', are small wild cats found mainly in South and Central America. They eat lots of different foods including rats, birds, frogs, monkeys, fish, tortoises and deer.

Think

How many types of food do you eat in a day? Is it as many as an ocelot?

What is the bounciest cat?

The bounciest cat is the African serval. It can leap one metre high and travel 4 metres as it jumps. Unusually, it hunts in the day, for frogs, locusts and voles. Servals are like cheetahs, with slim, graceful, spotty bodies.

Serval

Do cats change their coats?

The lynx changes its coat with the weather. It lives in forests in northern Europe and Asia. In summer, the lynx's coat is short and light-brown, but in winter its coat is much thicker, and light-grey. This helps it to hide throughout the year.

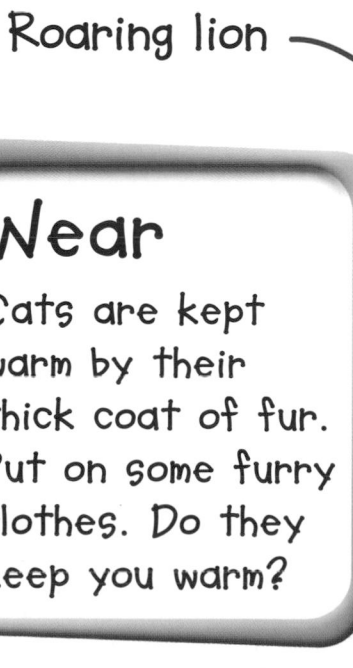

Why does a lion roar?

Lions roar to scare off other lions that stray onto their patch of land or territory. They also roar to let other members of their pride know where they are. A lion's roar is so loud it can be heard up to 10 kilometres away!

Roaring lion

Wear

Cats are kept warm by their thick coat of fur. Put on some furry clothes. Do they keep you warm?

Why do leopards climb trees?

Leopards climb trees to rest or to eat their food in safety. These big cats often kill prey that is larger than themselves. They are excellent climbers and are strong enough to drag their prey up into a tree, away from other hungry animals.

Leopard

Paint

Using face paints, ask an adult to make your face spotty like a leopard's.

How can humans help big cats?

Humans can help big cats by protecting areas of rainforest and grassland where they live. These areas are called 'reserves'. In a reserve, trees are not allowed to be cut down and the animals can live in safety.

Puma

No boat? Float!

In ancient times, Chinese soldiers used blown-up animal skins to cross deep rivers. They had to coat them with grease to keep the air in, and blow them up by mouth.

What is a puma's favourite food?

Rabbits, hares and rats are favourite foods for a puma. They will attack bigger animals too. In places where humans have built their homes near the puma's natural surroundings, people have been attacked by these cats.

How fast can a cheetah run?

Cheetahs are the world's fastest land animals. In a few seconds of starting a chase, a cheetah can reach its top speed of 105 kilometres an hour – as fast as a car! Cheetahs have 30 seconds to catch their prey before they run out of energy.

Why do people hunt big cats?

Mainly for their beautiful fur. For many years, cats have been killed in their hundreds of thousands so that people can wear their skins. Tigers especially were hunted for their body parts, which were used in Chinese medicines.

Make

With a paper plate and some straws for whiskers, make a tiger mask. Cut out eyeholes and paint it stripy!

Can't catch me!

Even though cheetahs are super-fast runners, only half of their chases end with a catch. Sometimes they scare their prey off before they get close enough to pounce.

Cheetah

Tiger

What time do tigers go hunting?

Almost all cats, including tigers, hunt at night. It is easier for a tiger to creep up on its prey when there is less light. A tiger may travel many kilometres each night while hunting. Tigers hunt deer, wild pigs, cattle and monkeys.

Which big cats live in grasslands?

Many big cats, including cheetahs, lions and leopards, live in grasslands called 'savannahs'. The savannah is dry, flat and open land, and is home to many other animals including gazelles, wildebeest and zebra. One of the best-known savannahs is the Serengeti in Africa.

Cheetahs hunting on the savannah

Cheetah cub

Play

With a friend, collect some pebbles and sticks and use them to mark out your own territories in your garden.

Why do cats wash their faces?

Cats wash their faces to spread their scent over their body. Cats have scent-producing body parts called glands on their chin. They use their paws to wipe the scent from their glands and when the cat walks, it can mark its area, or territory.

Slow down!

In the wild, cheetahs have a short lifespan. Their running speed gets a lot slower as they get older so they are less successful when they hunt.

How often do tigers eat?

Sometimes, tigers don't even eat once a week. When tigers catch an animal they can eat 40 kilograms of meat. They don't need to eat again for eight or nine days.

What is a group of cubs called?

A group of cubs is called a litter. There are usually between two and four cubs in every litter. Cubs need their mother's milk for the first few months, but gradually they start to eat meat. The young of some cats, such as the puma, are called kittens.

Mother puma and kittens

Sharpen your claws!

Unlike other cats, a cheetah's claws don't go back into its paws. This is why they don't often climb trees — they find it hard to get back down.

Leopards fighting

Why do leopards fight each other?

Leopards fight each other to defend their territory. Each leopard has its own patch of land, which it lives in. Leopards use scent-marking and make scratches on certain trees to warn other cats away, too. Sometimes, a fight will end in death.

Draw

Lots of other animals live in trees? Draw some pictures of animals that live in trees near you.

Which cat lives in the treetops?

Clouded leopards are excellent climbers and spend much of their time in the treetops of their forest home. These animals have been seen hanging upside-down from branches only by their back legs. Clouded leopards are brilliant swimmers, too.

Do big cats live in rainforests?

Jaguar

Yes, they do. Tigers and leopards live in rainforests in India, and jaguars live in South American rainforests. Here, the weather stays hot all year, although there is often lots of rain.

What animals do jaguars hunt?

Young jaguars climb trees to hunt for birds and small animals. As they grow bigger they get too heavy for the branches. Adult jaguars hunt on the ground for deer and small mammals, and sometimes cattle and horses.

How do cubs learn to hunt?

Cubs learn to hunt by playing. Even a tortoise is a fun toy and by playing like this, cubs learn hunting skills. Many mothers bring their cubs a small, live animal so they can practice catching it.

Think

Are you as playful as the lion cubs? Invent some new games of your own to play with your friends.

Lion cubs

It's a wrap!

The ancient Egyptians are well known for their 'mummies'. They even mummified animals including cats, birds and crocodiles.

How do snow leopards keep warm?

Snow leopards live on snowy mountains in Central Asia. To keep warm in winter they grow a thick coat of fur and store extra layers of fat under their skin. They also wrap their long tails around their bodies when they sleep to keep in heat.

Snow leopard →

Make

Paint a picture of your favourite big cat. Make it as colourful as you like and give your big cat a name.

Which cat goes fishing?

The jaguar is an expert at fishing. Sometimes it waves its tail over the water to trick hungry fish before it strikes. Jaguars also fish for turtles and tortoises. Their jaws are so powerful that they can easily crack open a turtle shell.

Jaguar

Snowshoes!

Siberian tigers have large padded paws. They act as snowshoes and stop the tiger from sinking into the snow as it walks.

How do tigers stay cool?

Tigers such as the Bengal tiger live in places where it gets extremely hot in the summer. They can often be seen laying in pools of water to cool off, or resting in a shady area out of the hot sun.

What is the most mysterious cat?

The clouded leopard is the most mysterious cat. It is so shy and rare that it is unusual to spot one. Clouded leopards grow to 2 metres in length, half of which is its tail. It uses its tail to balance as it leaps through the trees.

Clouded leopard

Why do cats always land on their feet?

Cats have bendy bodies and strong muscles. If a cat, such as a caracal, falls from a tree it can twist its body round so that it can land on its feet. Its muscles and joints take in the shock of the ground for a soft landing.

A caracal lands on its feet

How many babies do tigers have?

Tigers normally have between two and four babies called cubs. The mother tiger is pregnant for three months, and the cubs are born blind. Most births happen at night, probably because it is quieter and safer.

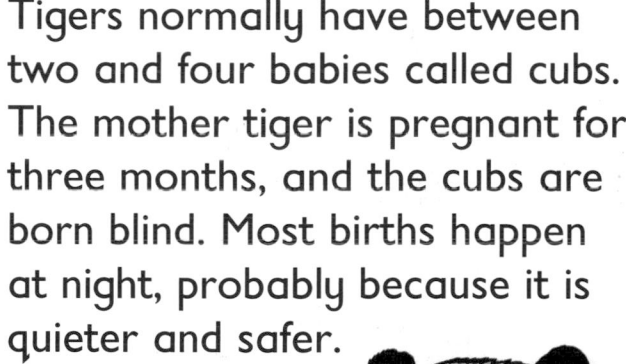

Measure

Using a measuring tape, see if you can measure how long a clouded leopard is.

Why are cats the perfect hunters?

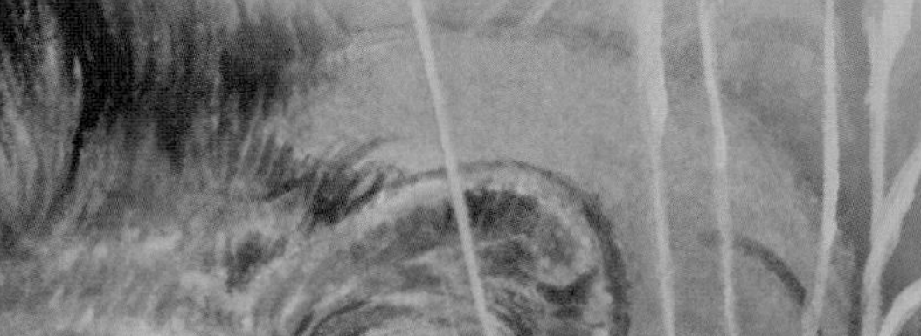

Because they have excellent eyesight and hearing, strong bodies and sharp teeth and claws. Many cats, such as lions, have fur that blends into their surroundings, which means they can hunt while staying hidden.

Lion hunting

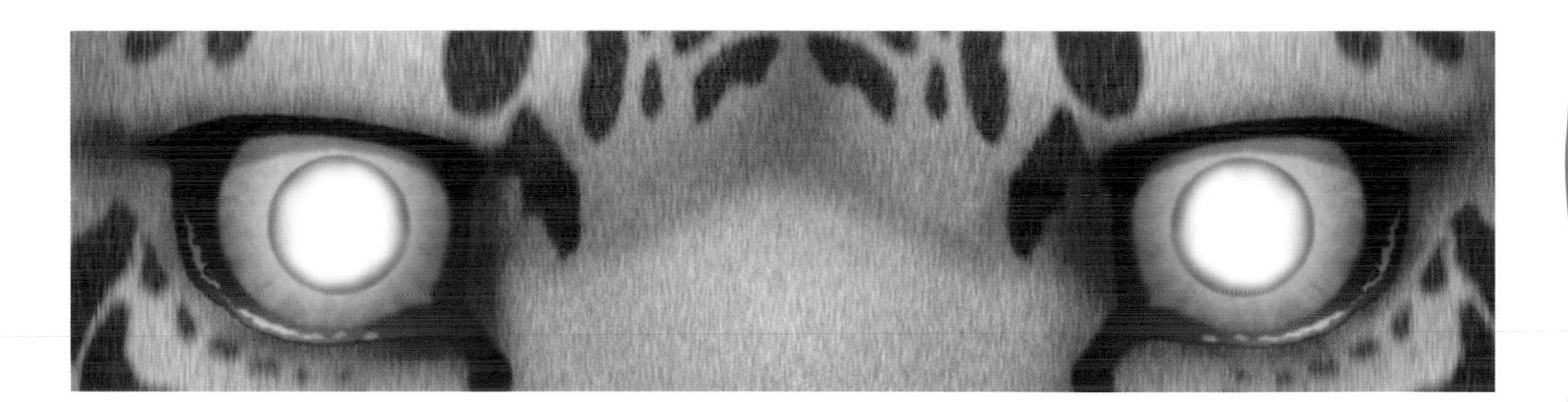

How do cats see in the dark?

Cats have special cells at the back of their eyes that reflect light. They are able to see objects clearly even in dim light, which is why many cats hunt at night. Cats can see four times better in the dark than humans can.

Try

How well can you see in the dark? Turn off the light and wait for your eyes to adjust. Can you see anything?

'Eye' can see you!

Cats have very good eyesight, in daylight and at night. For cats that live in grasslands, this helps them to spot distant prey on the open land.

Do big cats have enemies?

Big cats don't have many natural enemies. However, they watch out for animals, such as hyenas, that will gang up to steal their meal. A group of hyenas will attack and kill a big cat if it is weak or injured.

Quiz time

page 11

Do you remember what you have read about big cats? These questions will test your memory. The pictures will help you. If you get stuck, read the pages again.

3. Which cat is in danger?

page 11

4. What do ocelots eat?

page 4

1. What is the biggest cat?

page 12

5. What is the bounciest cat?

page 7

page 15

2. Are jaguars good swimmers?

6. How can humans help big cats?

7. Why do people hunt big cats?

page 16

page 26

11. What is the most mysterious cat?

8. What time do tigers go hunting?

page 17

12. How many babies do tigers have?

page 27

13. Do big cats have enemies?

page 29

9. Why do cats wash their faces?

page 19

10. Why do leopards fight each other?

page 21

Answers

1. The Siberian tiger
2. Yes, they are
3. The Iberian lynx
4. Rats, birds, frogs, monkeys, fish, tortoises and deer
5. The African serval
6. For their fur
7. By creating protected 'reserves'
8. At night
9. To spread scent over their body
10. To defend their territory
11. The clouded leopard
12. Between two and four babies, or cubs
13. No, but hyenas can be a threat

7. Why do people hunt big cats?

page 16

8. What time do tigers go hunting?

page 17

9. Why do cats wash their faces?

page 19

10. Why do leopards fight each other?

page 21

page 26

11. What is the most mysterious cat?

12. How many babies do tigers have?

page 27

13. Do big cats have enemies?

page 29

Answers

1. The Siberian tiger
2. Yes, they are
3. The Iberian lynx
4. Rats, birds, frogs, monkeys, fish, tortoises and deer
5. The African serval
6. For their fur
7. By creating protected 'reserves'
8. At night
9. To spread scent over their body
10. To defend their territory
11. The clouded leopard
12. Between two and four babies, or cubs
13. No, but hyenas can be a threat

Index